GRATITUDE JOURNAL & DEVOTIONAL

BECOMING PURPOSEFUL, PRAYERFUL, AND MINDFUL

By Jessica Lewis

© 2020 Jessica Lewis

All rights reserved. No part of this publication may be reproduced, stored in a retrieval system or transmitted in any form or by any means, electronic, mechanical, photocopying, recording or otherwise without the prior permission of the publisher or in accordance with the provisions of the Copyright, Designs and Patents Act 1988 or under the terms of any licence permitting limited copying issued by the Copyright Licensing Agency.

"Scripture quotations are from the ESV® Bible (The Holy Bible, English Standard Version®), copyright© 2001 by Crossway Bibles, a publishing ministry of Good News Publishers. Used by permission. All rights reserved."

Scripture quotations marked (NLT) are taken from the Holy Bible, New Living Translation, copyright © 1996, 2004, 2015 by Tyndale House Foundation. Used by permission of Tyndale House Publishers, a Division of Tyndale House Ministries, Carol Stream, Illinois 60188. All rights reserved.

Scripture quotations marked (NIV) are taken from the Holy Bible, New International Version®, NIV®. Copyright © 1973, 1978, 1984, 2011 by Biblica, Inc.™ Used by permission of Zondervan. All rights reserved worldwide. www.zondervan.com The "NIV" and "New International Version" are trademarks registered in the United States Patent and Trademark Office by Biblica, Inc.™

Scripture taken from the New King James Version®. Copyright © 1982 by Thomas Nelson. Used by permission. All rights reserved.

Scripture taken from the Holy Bible: International Standard Version®. Copyright © 1996-forever by The ISV Foundation. ALL RIGHTS RESERVED INTERNATIONALLY. Used by permission.

"Scripture quotations are from the ESV® Bible (The Holy Bible, English Standard Version®), copyright © 2001 by Crossway, a publishing ministry of Good News Publishers. Used by permission. All rights reserved."

"Scripture quotations taken from the New American Standard Bible® (NASB),

Copyright © 1960, 1962, 1963, 1968, 1971, 1972, 1973,

1975, 1977, 1995 by The Lockman Foundation

Used by permission. www.Lockman.org"

GOD'S WORD is a copyrighted work of God's Word to the Nations. Quotations are used by permission. Copyright 1995 by God's Word to the Nations. All rights reserved.

Scripture quotations marked CSB are been taken from the Christian Standard Bible®, Copyright © 2017 by Holman Bible Publishers. Used by permission. Christian Standard Bible•, and CSB® are federally registered trademarks of Holman Bible Publishers.

Typesetting: Kerry Ellis

Cover Design: Lucy Celebrates

A CIP record for this book is available from the Library of Congress Cataloging-in-Publication Data

ISBN: 978-1-952310-99-7

Printed by Corporate Color Printing Inc.

TIPS

TO GET THE MOST OUT OF THIS JOURNAL:

1 Commit to completing it regularly (preferably daily).

2 Be curious.

3 Prayerfully consider what God wants to show you through His Word.

4 Have fun!

My hope and intention is that this journal radically transforms how you view Jesus, the world, and yourself.

If this journal blesses your family and you want to order a copy for your niece, nephew, neighbor, youth group, friends or family visit: www.KidsGratitudeJournals.com

THIS JOURNAL BELONGS TO:

_____

DATE STARTED:

_____

Date: _____

Name 3 foods you
are grateful for:

1. _____

2. _____

3. _____

Verse of the Day

❝ *Then God said, 'I give you every seedbearing plant on the face of the whole earth and every tree that has fruit with seed in it. They will be yours for food.'*

Genesis 1:29 NIV

What does God want to show you from the verse of the day?

_____

_____

_____

Prayer

Thank you Lord for creating the Earth and everything you have blessed it with. Help me remember that all good things come from you.

Amen.

My Prayer

God, I need help with...

_____

_____

_____

Date: _____

Write 3 reasons why you
are grateful for your home:

1. _____

2. _____

3. _____

Verse of the Day

❝ *Therefore, everyone who hears these words of mine and puts them into practice is like a wise man who built his house on the rock.*

Matthew 7:24 NIV

What does God want to show you from the verse of the day?

_____

_____

_____

Prayer

Lord, thank you for the place I live. Help me follow your commandments, love you with all my heart, and listen to the words of the adults that care about me.

Amen

My Prayer

Lord, show me how to…

_____

_____

_____

Date: _____

Name 3 friends
you're grateful for:

1. _____

2. _____

3. _____

Verse of the Day

" Treat others the same way you want them to treat you.

Luke 6:31 NASB

What does God want to show you from the verse of the day?

_____

_____

_____

Prayer

Father in Heaven, thank you for my friends. Help me to treat them the way I would want to be treated.

Amen

My Prayer

God, help me be a better friend by...

_____

_____

_____

Date: _____

Write 3 reasons you are grateful for your parents, grandparents or family:

1. _____

2. _____

3. _____

Verse of the Day

❝ *Therefore, as God's chosen people, holy and dearly loved, clothe yourselves with compassion, kindness, humility, gentleness, and patience.*

Colossians 3:12 NIV

What does God want to show you from the verse of the day?

_____

_____

_____

Prayer

Father in Heaven, thank you for my friends. Help me to treat them the way I would want to be treated.

Amen

My Prayer

God, help me take the advice of _____ to

_____

_____

_____

Date: _____

Name 3 things in nature
you are grateful for:

1. _____

2. _____

3. _____

Verse of the Day

❝ The earth is the LORD's, and everything in it. The world and all its people belong to him. For he laid the earth's foundation on the seas and built it on the ocean depths.

Psalm 24:1-2 NIV

What does God want to show you from the verse of the day?

_____

_____

_____

Prayer

God, thank you for all the things you have created. Help me take care of the earth as you would.

Amen.

My Prayer

God, help me take better care of...

_____

_____

_____

Date: _____

Write 3 things about yourself
that you are grateful for:

1. _____

2. _____

3. _____

Verse of the Day

❝ *Then God said, 'Let us make mankind in our image, in our likeness, so that they may rule over the fish in the sea and the birds in the sky, over the livestock and all the wild animals, and over all the creatures that move along the ground.' So God created mankind in own image, in the image of God, He created them; male and female He created them.*

Genesis 1:26-27 NIV

What does God want to show you from the verse of the day?

_____

_____

_____

Prayer

Father in Heaven, thank you for creating me in your own image. Help me to see the special ways you made me different from everyone else.
Amen.

My Prayer

God, I thank you for making me good at...

_____

_____

_____

Date: _____

Name 3 things about God
you are grateful for:

1. _____

2. _____

3. _____

Verse of the Day

> *Our Lord and God, you are worthy to receive glory and honor and power, because you have created all things, and by your will they exist and were created.*
>
> Revelations 4:11 CSB

What does God want to show you from the verse of the day?

_____

_____

_____

Prayer

God, thank you for being patient, loving and providing all my needs. Help me grow closer to you every day.

Amen.

My Prayer

God, help me grow closer to you by...

_____

_____

_____

Date: _____

Write 3 things about a
mentor that you're grateful for:

1. _____

2. _____

3. _____

Verse of the Day

❝ *For everything that was written in the past was written to teach us, so that through the endurance taught in the Scriptures and the encouragement they provide we might have hope.*

Romans 15:4 NIV

What does God want to show you from the verse of the day?

_____

_____

_____

Prayer

God, thank you for _____. Thank you for the time, attention, and ways they help me to learn new things.

My Prayer

God, help me to be at...

_____

_____

_____

Date: _____

Write 3 things that happened
yesterday that you're grateful for:

1. _____

2. _____

3. _____

Verse of the Day

❝ If we confess our sins, he is faithful

and righteous to forgive us our

sins, and to cleanse us from all

unrighteousness.

1 John 1:9 ESV

What does God want to show you from the verse of the day?

_____

_____

_____

Prayer

God, thank you for forgiving me for my sins. Help me to ask for forgiveness when I do things I should not.

Amen.

My Prayer

God, forgive me for...

_____

_____

_____

Date: _____

Name 3 people you are grateful for:

1. _____

2. _____

3. _____

Verse of the Day

> *The righteous choose their friends carefully, but the way of the wicked leads them astray.*
>
> Proverbs 12:26 NIV

What does God want to show you from the verse of the day?

_____

_____

_____

Prayer

God, thank you for my friends. Help me choose friends that are a good influence for me.

Amen.

My Prayer

God, the friends you would want me to have are...

_____

_____

_____

Date: _____

Name 3 people you
are grateful for:

1. _____

2. _____

3. _____

Verse of the Day

❝ *The righteous choose their friends carefully, but the way of the wicked leads them astray.*

Proverbs 12:26 NIV

What does God want to show you from the verse of the day?

_____

_____

_____

Prayer

God, thank you for my friends. Help me choose friends that are a good influence for me.

Amen.

My Prayer

God, the friends you would want me to have are...

_____

_____

_____

Date: _____

Name 3 places you
are grateful for:

1. _____

2. _____

3. _____

Verse of the Day

" I have told you these things, so that in me you may have peace. In this world you will have trouble. But take heart! I have overcome the world.

John 16:33 NIV

What does God want to show you from the verse of the day?

_____

_____

_____

Prayer

Father in heaven, thank you for giving me peace. Help me to pray when I feel unsettled or uneasy.
Amen.

My Prayer

God, I need your peace and want to feel better about...

_____

_____

_____

Date: _____

Name 3 things in your room
that you are grateful for:

1. _____

2. _____

3. _____

Verse of the Day

" *If someone has enough money to live well and sees a brother or sister in need but shows no compassion—how can God's love be in that person?*

1 John 3:17 NLT

What does God want to show you from the verse of the day?

_____

_____

_____

Prayer

God, thank you for everything I have. Help me to help others that are in need.

Amen.

My Prayer

God, a person I can help is…

_____

By…

_____

Date: _____

Name 3 people in your
family you are grateful for:

1. _____

2. _____

3. _____

Verse of the Day

❝ *The spirit himself testifies with our spirit that we are God's children.*

Romans 8:16 NIV

What does God want to show you from the verse of the day?

_____

_____

_____

Prayer

God, thank you for making me yours. Help me to feel your love and presence every day of my life.

Amen.

My Prayer

God, help me to love others by...

_____

_____

_____

Date: _____

Write 3 reasons you are grateful for your body:

1. _____

2. _____

3. _____

Verse of the Day

> Don't you realize that your body is the temple of the Holy Spirit, who lives in you and was given to you by God? You do not belong to yourself, for God bought you with a high price. So you must honor God with your body.

1 Corinthians 6:19-20 NLT

What does God want to show you from the verse of the day?

_____

_____

_____

Prayer

Thank you for creating my body the way it is. Help me to see myself as you do.

Amen.

My Prayer

God, help me to take better care of my body by…

_____

_____

_____

Date: _____

Name 3 people you love
and are grateful for:

1. _____

2. _____

3. _____

Verse of the Day

> Then Christ will make his home in your hearts as you trust in Him. Your roots will grow down into God's love and keep you strong. And may you have the power to understand, as all God's people should, how wide, how long, how high, and how deep his love is.

Ephesians 3:17-18 NLT

What does God want to show you from the verse of the day?

_____

_____

_____

Prayer

Lord, thank you for your constant love. Help me to pray and ask for your love when I need it.

Amen.

My Prayer

Lord, help me act more loving and kind to...

_____

By...

_____

_____

Date: _____

Write 3 ways God made you different from everyone else:

1. _____

2. _____

3. _____

Verse of the Day

❝ *God saved you by his grace when you believed. And you can't take credit for this; it is a gift from God. Salvation is not a reward for the good things we have done, so none of us can boast about it.*

Ephesians 2:8-9 NLT

What does God want to show you from the verse of the day?

_____

_____

_____

Prayer

God, thank you for creating me different than everyone else. Help me to see myself through your eyes; perfect, loved, special, unique, and gifted.

Amen.

My Prayer

God, when I see people that are different than me I…

_____

_____

Help me to…

_____

Date: _____

Name 3 sweet things
you're grateful for:

1. _____

2. _____

3. _____

Verse of the Day

❝ *Kind words are like a honeycomb, sweet to the soul and healing to the bones.*

Proverbs 16:24 NLT

What does God want to show you from the verse of the day?

___

___

___

Prayer

God, thank you for words and the power they have. Help me to use words that lift others up.

Amen.

My Prayer

God, the person I want to encourage is....

___

by...

___

___

Date: _____

Name 3 feelings you
are grateful for:

1. _____

2. _____

3. _____

Verse of the Day

❝ Don't worry about anything; instead, pray about everything. Tell God what you need, and thank Him for all He has done.

Philippians 4:6 NLT

What does God want to show you from the verse of the day?

_____

_____

_____

Prayer

God, thank you for always being available for me to pray to. Lord, remind me to pray in all situations: when I am happy, sad, worried, joyful or angry.

Amen

My Prayer

God, I worry about...

_____

_____

Help me to pray when I start to worry.
_____

Date: _____

Write 3 of your
favorite Bible stories:

1. _____

2. _____

3. _____

Verse of the Day

" You will seek me and find me when you search for me with all your heart.

Jeremiah 29:13 ISV

What does God want to show you from the verse of the day?

_____

_____

_____

Prayer

God, thank you for the Bible and making yourself known to me through the stories that are in it. Help me to read your stories and understand more about you each time.

Amen.

My Prayer

God, I only read the Bible when…

_____

_____

Help me read it…

_____

Date: _____

Name 3 things that are hot or warm that you are grateful for:

1. _____

2. _____

3. _____

Verse of the Day

❝ *If you forgive those who sin against you, your heavenly Father will forgive you. But if you refuse to forgive others, your Father will not forgive your sins.*

Matthew 6:14-15 NLT

What does God want to show you from the verse of the day?

_____

_____

_____

Prayer

Father in heaven, thank you for sending your son Jesus to die on the cross and raising Him back to life, so that my sins may be forgiven. Help me to forgive others as you have forgiven me.

Amen.

My Prayer

God, I forgive...

_____

For...

_____

_____

Date: _____

Write 3 reasons you are grateful for water:

1. _____
2. _____
3. _____

Verse of the Day

" *Then Moses raised his hand over the sea, and the Lord opened up a path through the water with a strong east wind. The wind blew all that night, turning the seabed into dry land. So the people of Israel walking through the middle of the sea on dry ground, with walls of water on each side!*

Exodus 14:21-22 NLT

What does God want to show you from the verse of the day?

_____

_____

_____

Prayer

God, thank you for stories like this, stories that show me how much you love your people. Lord, help me to see your love and compassion as I read the Bible.

Amen.

My Prayer

God, I doubt you when…

_____

Give me greater belief in…

_____

_____

Date: _____

Write 3 reasons you
are grateful for food:

1. _____

2. _____

3. _____

Verse of the Day

❝ But Jesus told him, 'No! The Scriptures say, 'People do not live by bread alone, but by every word that comes from the mouth of God.

Matthew 4:4 NLT

What does God want to show you from the verse of the day?

_____

_____

_____

Prayer

God, thank you for your teachings in the Bible. Help me to see that your commandments are to keep me safe from all my challenges and temptations, and not to limit what I can do.

Amen.

My Prayer

God, forgive me for...

_____

_____

_____

Date: _____

Write 3 reasons you are grateful
for your home or place you live:

1. _____

2. _____

3. _____

Verse of the Day

" Know that the LORD your God is God, the trusted God who faithfully keeps his covenant to the thousandth generation of those who love him and obey his commands.

Deuteronomy 7:9 ISV

The 10 Commandments:

1. Love God more than anything else
2. Don't make anything more important than God
3. Always say God's name with love and respect
4. Honor God by resting on the 7th day of the week
5. Love and respect your mom and dad
6. Never murder anyone
7. Always be faithful to your husband or wife
8. Don't take anything that isn't yours
9. Always tell the truth
10. Be happy with what you have. Don't wish to have other people's things.

Prayer

God, thank you for showing me how to live according to your commandments.

My Prayer

God, the commandments I need the most help with are...

_____

_____

_____

Date: _____

Write 3 reasons you are grateful for your church or a Christian leader:

1. _____

2. _____

3. _____

Verse of the Day

❝ *The fear of the LORD is the beginning of knowledge, But fools despise wisdom and instruction.*

Proverbs 1:7 NKJV

What does God want to show you from the verse of the day?

_____

_____

_____

Prayer

God, thank you for the positive influences in my life. Help me to stay thankful for all I get to learn every day.

Amen.

My Prayer

God, help me to be a better learner by...

_____

_____

_____

Date: _____

Name 3 things in your house
that you are grateful for:

1. _____

2. _____

3. _____

Verse of the Day

❝ We know that all things work together for the good of those who love God- those whom He has called according to his plan.

Romans 8:28 GW

What does God want to show you from the verse of the day?

_____

_____

_____

Prayer

God, thank you for working to make all things for my good. Help me to remember that you are in control always.

Amen.

My Prayer

God, I worry about...

_____

_____

Help me to pray and trust that you will handle it all.

Date: _____

Name 3 animals in the sea
you are grateful for:

1. _____

2. _____

3. _____

Verse of the Day

❝ *Then God said, 'Let the water swarm with living creatures, and let birds fly above the earth across the expanse of the sky.' So God created the large sea-creatures and every living creature that moves and swarms in the water, according to their kinds. He also created every winged creature according to its kind. And God saw that it was good.*

Genesis 1:20-21 CSB

What does God want to show you from the verse of the day?

_____

_____

_____

Prayer

God, thank you for creating animals. Help me to see your creativity and vast imagination when I see animals.

Amen.

My Prayer

God, help to be more creative by...

_____

_____

_____

Date: _____

Name 3 things that fly
that you are grateful for:

1. _____

2. _____

3. _____

Verse of the Day

❝ *God blessed them; and said to them, 'Be fruitful and multiply, and fill the earth, and subdue it; rule over the fish of the sea and over the birds of the sky and over every living thing that moves on the earth.'*

Genesis 1:28 NASB

What does God want to show you from the verse of the day?

_____

_____

_____

Prayer

God, thank you for giving me the ability to care for the things that you have created. Show me ways I can care for your creation just as you would.

Amen.

My Prayer

God, I want to take better care of...

_____

_____

_____

Date: _____

Name 3 things that grow that you are grateful for:

1. _____

2. _____

3. _____

Verse of the Day

> And He said to him, 'YOU SHALL LOVE THE LORD YOUR GOD WITH ALL YOUR HEART, AND WITH ALL YOUR SOUL, AND WITH ALL YOUR MIND.' This is the great and foremost commandment. The second is like it, 'YOU SHALL LOVE YOUR NEIGHBOR AS YOURSELF.'

Matthew 22:37-39 NASB

What does God want to show you from the verse of the day?

_____

_____

_____

Prayer

Lord, thank you for teaching me how to live and treat others right. Help me to love you above everything else in this world.

Amen.

My Prayer

God, I love you because...

_____

_____

_____

Date: _____

Name 3 noises or sounds
that you are grateful for:

1. _____

2. _____

3. _____

Verse of the Day

> *Every good present and every perfect gift comes from above, from the Father who made the sun, moon, and stars. The Fathers doesn't change like the shifting shadows produced by the sun and the moon.*

James 1:17 GW

What does God want to show you from the verse of the day?

___

___

___

Prayer

God, thank you for allowing me to hear sounds. Help me to praise and worship you daily with my own voice.

Amen.

My Prayer

God, help me this week with...

___

___

___

CHECK IN POINT

GO BACK AND SEE:

What prayers has God answered?

_____
_____
_____
_____

What prayers do you need to continue to pray?

_____
_____
_____
_____

How are you thinking different
since starting this journal?

_____

_____

_____

How are you acting different
since starting this journal?

_____

_____

_____

_____

Date: _____

Write 3 reasons you're grateful for today:

1. _____

2. _____

3. _____

Verse of the Day

❝ *'For I know the plans I have for you,' declares the Lord, 'plans to prosper you and not to harm you, plans to give you hope and a future. Then you will call on me and come and pray to me and I will listen to you.'*

Jeremiah 29:11-12 NIV

What does God want to show you from the verse of the day?

_____

_____

_____

Prayer

Lord, thank you for the hope you have given me. Help me to pray when things are hard and when things are good.

Amen.

My Prayer

Lord, I need you when…

_____

_____

_____

Date: _____

Name 3 things that smell good
that you are grateful for:

1. _____

2. _____

3. _____

Verse of the Day

" *May the God of hope fill you with all joy and peace as you trust in Him, so that you may overflow with hope by the power of the Holy Spirit.*

Romans 15:13 NIV

What does God want to show you from the verse of the day?

_____

_____

_____

Prayer

God, thank you for giving me the ability to smell and taste the amazing food you provide me with.

Amen.

My Prayer

God, help me trust you with...

_____

_____

_____

Date: _____

Name 3 places you
are grateful for:

1. _____
2. _____
3. _____

Verse of the Day

❝ Give thanks to the Lord, proclaim his name; make known among the nations what He has done. Sing to Him, sing praise to Him; tell of all his wonderful acts.

1 Chronicles 16:8-9 NIV

What does God want to show you from the verse of the day?

_____

_____

_____

Prayer

Lord, thank you for all the different cities and places you have created. Help me to think of you and give you all the glory and wonder as I am given opportunities to visit new places.

Amen.

My Prayer

Lord, I normally praise you when...

_____

Help me to praise you...

_____

Date: _____

Write 3 things that
you're grateful you can do:

1. _____

2. _____

3. _____

Verse of the Day

❝ *But those who trust in the LORD will renew their strength; they will soar on wings like eagles; they will run and not become weary, they will walk and not faint.*

Isaiah 40:31 CSB

What does God want to show you from the verse of the day?

_____

_____

_____

Prayer

Lord, thank you for the strength you have given me. Help me to see and know that all my strength, gifts, and talent come from you.

Amen.

My Prayer

Lord, I need your strength with…

_____

_____

_____

Date: _____

Name 3 things you've done with your family or friends that you're grateful for:

1. _____

2. _____

3. _____

Verse of the Day

❝ *There is nothing better for a person than to eat, drink and enjoy his work. I have seen that even this is from God's hand, because who can eat and who can enjoy life apart from Him?*

Ecclesiastes 2:24-25 CSB

What does God want to show you from the verse of the day?

___

___

Prayer

Lord, I thank you for giving the ability to eat and drink with the people I love. Help me to appreciate the people around me even more.

Amen.

My Prayer

Lord, I don't enjoy …

___

Help me to…

___

Date: _____

Name 3 things about God
that you are grateful for:

1. _____

2. _____

3. _____

Verse of the Day

❝ *I can do all things through Christ who strengthens me.*

Philippians 4:13 NKJV

What does God want to show you
from the verse of the day?

_____

_____

_____

Prayer

God, thank you for the forgiveness and patience that you have given me. Thank you for calling me your child and loving me like no one else can.

Amen.

My Prayer

God, give me patience with...

_____

_____

_____

Date: _____

Name 3 movies you
are grateful for:

1. _____

2. _____

3. _____

Verse of the Day

" *Give thanks to the Lord, for he is good; his love endures forever.*

Psalm 107:1 NIV

What does God want to show you from the verse of the day?

___

___

___

Prayer

Lord, thank you for your unending love. Help me to love you above everything else.

Amen.

My Prayer

Lord, help me spend more time with you by...

___

___

___

Date: _____

Write 3 reasons why you
are grateful for your hands:

1. _____

2. _____

3. _____

Verse of the Day

" Your right hand, O LORD, is glorious in power. Your right hand, O LORD, smashes the enemy..

Exodus 15:6 NLT

What does God want to show you from the verse of the day?

_____

_____

_____

Prayer

God, thank you for creating me in your image.
Thank you for making me unique and special.

Amen.

My Prayer

God, thank you for making me special by...

_____

_____

_____

Date: _____

Write 3 reasons why you
are grateful for your eyes:

1. _____

2. _____

3. _____

Verse of the Day

> You made all the delicate, inner parts of my body and knit me together in my mother's womb. Thank you for making me so wonderfully complex! Your workmanship is marvelous—how well I know it.
>
> Psalm 139:13-14 NLT

What does God want to show you from the verse of the day?

_____

_____

_____

Prayer

God, thank you for my ability to see. Help me to see people and be kind to them as you do.

Amen.

My Prayer

God, I will be kinder to...

_____

By...

_____

_____

Date: _____

Write 3 reasons why you are grateful for the city or town you live in:

1. _____

2. _____

3. _____

Verse of the Day

> O LORD, you have examined my heart and know everything about me. You know when I sit down or stand up. You know my thoughts even when I'm far away. You see me when I travel and when I rest at home. You know everything I do.

Psalm 139:1-3 NLT

What does God want to show you from the verse of the day?

_____

_____

_____

Prayer

God, thank you for the place I live. Help me to fill it with things that are good and pleasing to you.

Amen.

My Prayer

God, help me to stop...

_____

_____

_____

Date: _____

Write 3 things that happen during the morning that you are grateful for:

1. _____

2. _____

3. _____

Verse of the Day

❝ *Let the morning bring me word of your unfailing love, for I have put my trust in you. Show me the way I should go, for to you I entrust my life. Rescue me from my enemies, LORD, for I hide myself in you.*

Psalm 143:8-9 NIV

What does God want to show you from the verse of the day?

_____

_____

_____

Prayer

God, thank you for the good and bad things that happen in my life. Help me to trust that all things work out for good, for those who love you.

Amen.

My Prayer

God, I don't understand why you allow...

_____

Help me...

_____

_____

Date: _____

Write 3 things that happen at night that you are grateful for:

1. _____

2. _____

3. _____

Verse of the Day

" *And God said, 'Let there be light,' and there was light. God saw that the light was good, and he separated the light from the darkness. God called the light 'day,' and the darkness he called 'night'. And there was evening, and there was morning- the first day.*

Genesis 1:3-5 NIV

What does God want to show you from the verse of the day?

_____

_____

_____

Prayer

God, thank you for the stars in the sky. Help me to feel wrapped in your love, peace, and presence when I go to sleep tonight. Help me to feel secure by knowing you are looking over me.

Amen.

My Prayer

God, I get scared of...

_____

Help me...

_____

_____

Date: _____

Write 3 reasons why you
are grateful for the Earth:

1. _____

2. _____

3. _____

Verse of the Day

> In the beginning God created the heavens and the earth. The earth was formless and empty, and darkness covered the deep waters. And the Spirit of God was hovering over the surface of the waters.

Genesis 1:1-2 NLT

What does God want to show you from the verse of the day?

_____

_____

_____

Prayer

God, thank you for the ocean and everything in it. Help me treat and care for the earth as you would want me to, with kindness and love.

Amen.

My Prayer

God, I will take better care of the Earth by...

_____

_____

_____

Date: _____

Write 3 reasons why you
are grateful for winter time:

1. _____

2. _____

3. _____

Verse of the Day

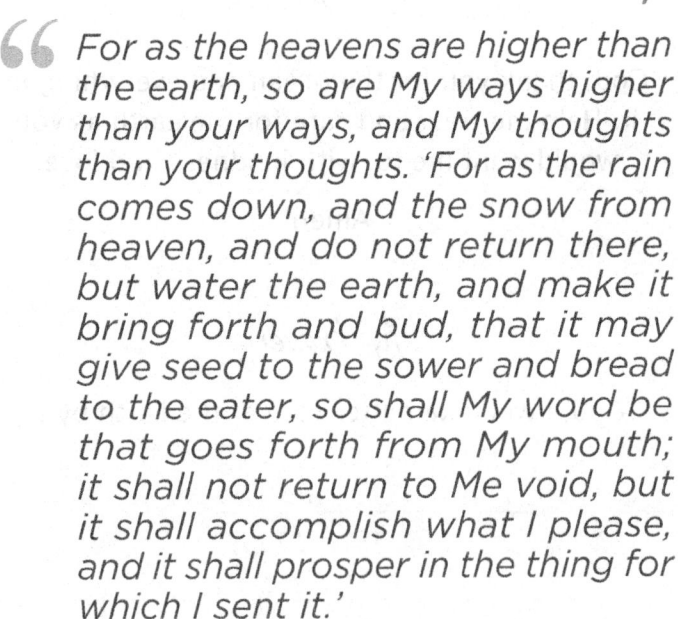

" For as the heavens are higher than the earth, so are My ways higher than your ways, and My thoughts than your thoughts. 'For as the rain comes down, and the snow from heaven, and do not return there, but water the earth, and make it bring forth and bud, that it may give seed to the sower and bread to the eater, so shall My word be that goes forth from My mouth; it shall not return to Me void, but it shall accomplish what I please, and it shall prosper in the thing for which I sent it.'

Isaiah 55:9-11 NKJV

What does God want to show you from the verse of the day?

_____

_____

_____

Prayer

God, thank you for the different seasons and temperatures. Help me to be reminded of your greatness when I see a flower blooming or a fallen leaf.

Amen.

My Prayer

God, help me act differently when...

_____

_____

_____

Date: _____

Write 3 reasons why you
are grateful for summer time:

1. _____

2. _____

3. _____

Verse of the Day

" Look at the birds. They don't plant or harvest or store food in barns, for your heavenly Father feeds them. And aren't you far more valuable to him than they are? Can all your worries add a single moment to your life?

Matthew 6:26-27 NLT

What does God want to show you from the verse of the day?

_____

_____

_____

Prayer

Heavenly Father, thank you for the fun I have in the summertime. Help me to give all my worries to you. Fill me with your peace.

Amen.

My Prayer

Heavenly Father, I worry about...

_____

When I begin to worry, help me...

_____

_____

Date: _____

Write 3 reasons why you
are grateful for your birthday:

1. _____

2. _____

3. _____

Verse of the Day

" For we are God's masterpiece. He has created us anew in Christ Jesus, so we can do the good things he planned for us long ago.

Ephesians 2:10 NLT

What does God want to show you from the verse of the day?

_____

_____

_____

Prayer

Lord, thank you for my life. Help me to fully understand that I am your precious masterpiece.

Amen.

My Prayer

Lord, help me to be the best person I can be by…

_____

_____

_____

Date: _____

Write 3 things that you are grateful for that happened in the last week:

1. _____

2. _____

3. _____

Verse of the Day

❝ *This is how God's love was revealed among us: God sent his unique Son into the world so that we might live through him. This is love: not that we have loved God, but that he loved us and sent his Son to be the atoning sacrifice for our sins. Dear friends, if this is the way God loved us, we must also love one another.*

1 John 4:9-11 ISV

What does God want to show you from the verse of the day?

_____

_____

_____

Prayer

God, thank you for sending your one and only son, Jesus, to die on the cross to forgive my sins. Help me forgive others as you have forgiven me.

Amen.

My Prayer

God, I forgive...

_____

For...

_____

_____

Date: _____

Write 3 things that you have learned in school that you are grateful for:

1. _____

2. _____

3. _____

Verse of the Day

❝ *The fear of the LORD is the beginning of knowledge, But fools despise wisdom and instruction.*

Proverbs 1:7 NKJV

What does God want to show you from the verse of the day?

_____

_____

_____

Prayer

Lord, thank you for my brain and my ability to learn. Help me to stay humble and open to learning more about you.

Amen.

My Prayer

Lord, I don't listen to...

_____

I will...

_____

_____

Date: _____

Write 3 things about your brain that you are grateful for:

1. _____
2. _____
3. _____

Verse of the Day

❝ *For the Lord grants wisdom! From his mouth come knowledge and understanding. He grants a treasure of common sense to the honest. He is a shield to those who walk with integrity. He guards the paths of the just and protects those who are faithful to Him.*

Proverbs 2:6-8 NLT

What does God want to show you from the verse of the day?

_____

_____

_____

Prayer

Lord, thank you for protecting my path. Help me be honest and do what is right, even when no one is watching and even when it is hard.

Amen.

My Prayer

Lord, I haven't been honest about...

_____

_____

_____

Date: _____

Name 3 things that are
outside you are grateful for:

1. _____

2. _____

3. _____

Verse of the Day

❝ In his hands are the depths of the earth; the heights of the mountains are his also. The sea is his, for He made it, and his hands formed the dry land.

Psalm 95:4-5 ESV

What does God want to show you from the verse of the day?

_____

_____

_____

Prayer

Lord, thank you for all you have created, including me. Help me begin to understand all you have done and continue to do for me. Help me to realize that you are by my side every day.

Amen.

My Prayer

God, I am most excited about...

_____

Help me...

_____

_____

Date: _____

Name 3 things that are round
that you are grateful for:

1. _____

2. _____

3. _____

Verse of the Day

" Don't become like the people of this world. Instead, change the way you think. Then you will always be able to determine what God really wants- what is good, pleasing, and perfect.

Romans 12:2 GW

What does God want to show you from the verse of the day?

_____

_____

_____

Prayer

God, thank you for my mind and my ability to learn. Help me to learn and follow the ways you want me to live so I can follow your commands for me.

Amen.

My Prayer

God, I need help with...

_____

_____

_____

Date: _____

Name 3 parts of your body
that you are grateful for:

1. _____

2. _____

3. _____

Verse of the Day

❝ *We have different gifts, according to the grace given to each of us. If your gift is prophesying, then prophesy in accordance with your faith; if it is serving, then serve; if it is teaching, then teach; if it is to encourage, then give encouragement; if it is giving, then give generously; if it is to lead, do it diligently; if it is to show mercy, do it cheerfully.*

Romans 12:6-8 NIV

What does God want to show you from the verse of the day?

_____

_____

_____

Prayer

God, thank you for the things I am good at and the talent you have given me. Help me to use my gifts to serve you and others.

Amen.

My Prayer

God, help me become better at...

_____

_____

_____

Date: _____

Write 3 reasons you
are grateful for food:

1. _____

2. _____

3. _____

Verse of the Day

❝ Jesus replied, 'I am the bread of life. Whoever comes to me will never be hungry again. Whoever believes in my will never be thirsty.'.

John 6:35 NLT

What does God want to show you from the verse of the day?

_____

_____

_____

Prayer

God, thank you for the food you have provided. Help me to eat healthy foods that are good for my body.

Amen.

My Prayer

God, help me have better self-control with...

_____

_____

_____

Date: _____

What are 3 things that make you laugh that you are grateful for:

1. _____

2. _____

3. _____

Verse of the Day

" *Our mouths were filled with laughter then, and our tongues with shouts of joy. Then they said among the nations, "The LORD has done great things for them.*

Psalm 126:2 CSB

What does God want to show you from the verse of the day?

_____

_____

_____

Prayer

God, thank you for my joy and happiness. Help me to find more joy in learning about you.

Amen.

My Prayer

God, when I sing worship songs, help me to...

_____

_____

_____

Date: _____

What are 3 fun things
you are grateful for:

1. _____

2. _____

3. _____

Verse of the Day

> Whatever you do, do it from the heart, as something done for the Lord and not for people...

Colossians 3:23 CSB

What does God want to show you from the verse of the day?

_____

_____

_____

Prayer

God, thank you for the fun I have had. Help me to do all things for you, rather than for the approval of my friends.

Amen.

My Prayer

God, if someone talks bad about me I...

_____

Help me know that, no matter what my friends think of me, you love me and your love is what matters.

Date: _____

Name 3 soft things that
you are grateful for:

1. _____

2. _____

3. _____

Verse of the Day

❝ Be kind to one another, tenderhearted, forgiving one another, as God in Christ forgave you.

Ephesians 4:32 ESV

What did you learn from the verse of the day?

_____

_____

_____

Prayer

God, thank you for all the people in my life. Help me to treat people just like you would treat them.

Amen.

My Prayer

God, I will treat _____ better by...

_____

_____

Date: _____

Name 3 hard things
you are grateful for:

1. _____

2. _____

3. _____

Verse of the Day

❝ Consider it a great joy, my brothers and sisters, whenever you experience various trials, because you know that the testing of your faith produces endurance.

James 1:2-3 CSB

What does God want to show you from the verse of the day?

_____

_____

_____

Prayer

God, thank you for the challenges I face in my life. Although challenges may not be easy to overcome, you promise to work them out for good for those who love you. Help me to be faithful and strong.

My Prayer

God, a challenge I need help with is...

_____

_____

_____

Date: _____

Name 3 things with wheels that you are grateful for:

1. _____

2. _____

3. _____

Verse of the Day

❝ *No one undergoing a trial should say, 'I am being tempted by God,' since God is not tempted by evil, and He himself does not tempt anyone.*

James 1:13 CSB

What does God want to show you from the verse of the day?

_____

_____

_____

Prayer

God, thank you for not tempting me, instead making me strong. Help me and give me self-control when I want to do things I know I shouldn't.

My Prayer

God, I feel tempted by...

_____

Help me...

_____

_____

Date: _____

Name 3 green things
that you are grateful for:

1. _____

2. _____

3. _____

Verse of the Day

❝ Let us come into his presence with thanksgiving; let us make a joyful noise to him with songs of praise! For the LORD is a great God, and a great King above all gods. He holds in his hands the depths of the earth and the mightiest mountains. The sea belongs to him, for he made it. His hands formed the dry land, too.

Psalm 95:2-5 ESV

What does God want to show you from the verse of the day?

_____

_____

_____

Prayer

Lord, thank you for giving me shelter. Help me to see the mountains, the sea, and the lands and be reminded that you created it all.

Amen.

My Prayer

Lord, I have been ungrateful for...

_____

Help me to...

_____

_____

CHECK IN POINT

LOOK BACK THROUGH THE LAST 30 ENTRIES:

What prayers has God answered?

_____

_____

_____

What prayers do you need to continue to pray?

_____

_____

_____

Do you find yourself more
grateful throughout your day?
For what?

_____

_____

_____

_____

How is this journal changing
the way you think and act?

_____

_____

_____

_____

Date: _____

Name 3 red things
you are grateful for:

1. _____

2. _____

3. _____

Verse of the Day

❝ But as it is written,

What no eye has seen, no ear has heard, and no human heart has conceived- God has prepared these things for those who love him.

1 Corinthians 2:9 CSB

What does God want to show you from the verse of the day?

_____

_____

_____

Prayer

God, thank you for all you have planned for me. Help me to trust you and pray in all good and difficult situations.

Amen.

My Prayer

God, I don't understand why...

_____

_____

_____

Date: _____

What are 3 reasons you
are grateful to be alive:

1. _____

2. _____

3. _____

Verse of the Day

> Therefore, I tell you, whatever you ask for in prayer, believe that you have received it, and it will be yours.

Mark 11:24 NIV

What does God want to show you from the verse of the day?

_____

_____

_____

Prayer

God, thank you for hearing all my prayers. Help me to wait patiently when you choose not to answer them the way I was hoping for.

Amen.

My Prayer

God, a prayer you haven't answered yet is...

_____

Help me to...

_____

_____

Date: _____

Name 3 yummy foods
you are grateful for:

1. _____

2. _____

3. _____

Verse of the Day

❝ *Give, and it will be given to you; a good measure--pressed down, shaken together, and running over--will be poured into your lap. For with the measure you use, it will be measured back to you.*

Luke 6:38 CSB

What does God want to show you from the verse of the day?

_____

_____

_____

Prayer

God, thank you for your fairness. You are the same yesterday, today, and forever. Help me to hear your lessons about being generous and become more generous like you.

Amen.

My Prayer

God, I can be more generous by...

_____

_____

_____

Date: _____

Write 3 reasons you are grateful
to be a member of your family:

1. _____

2. _____

3. _____

Verse of the Day

❝ Peter began to speak: "Now I truly understand that God doesn't show favoritism, but in every nation the person who fears him and does what is right is acceptable to him.

Acts 10:34-35 CSB

What does God want to show you from the verse of the day?

Prayer

God, thank you for guiding me and helping me to do the right thing. Please continue to help me to make good decisions that please you.

Amen.

My Prayer

God, help me…

Date: _____

Write 3 reasons you are
grateful for a friend:

1. _____

2. _____

3. _____

Verse of the Day

> *Jesus replied, 'All who love me will do what I say. My Father will love them, and we will come and make our home with each of them. Anyone who doesn't love me will not obey me.'*

John 14:23-24 NLT

What does God want to show you from the verse of the day?

_____

_____

_____

Prayer

Father in heaven, thank you for giving me the exact ways to follow you; your commandments. Give me self-control and strength to follow them.

Amen.

My Prayer

Father in heaven, I need your help following the commandment that says...

_____

_____

_____

Date: _____

What are 3 reasons you
are grateful for your nose:

1. _____

2. _____

3. _____

Verse of the Day

❝ Don't just pretend to love others. Really love them. Hate what is wrong. Hold tightly to what is good.

Romans 12:9 NLT

What does God want to show you from the verse of the day?

_____

_____

_____

Prayer

God, thank you for the love you give me.
I am so thankful to be your child. Help
me to love others as you would.

Amen.

My Prayer

God, I will love my family better by...

_____

_____

_____

Date: _____

What are 3 reasons you are grateful to be the age that you are:

1. _____

2. _____

3. _____

Verse of the Day

" *Rejoice in our confident hope. Be patient in trouble, and keep on praying.*

Romans 12:12 NLT

What does God want to show you from the verse of the day?

_____

_____

_____

Prayer

God, thank you for all I have to be happy about in life. Help me to be patient when things don't go the way I want them to. Help me to spread your joy during my day.

Amen.

My Prayer

God, I need more patience with…

_____

_____

_____

Date: _____

Name 3 lunchtime foods
you are grateful for:

1. _____

2. _____

3. _____

Verse of the Day

❝ *Everyone who calls on the name of the Lord will be saved.*

Romans 10:13 NIV

What does God want to show you from the verse of the day?

_____

_____

_____

Prayer

Lord, thank you for providing the healthy food that nourishes my body. Help me to be thankful for all that I have.

Amen.

My Prayer

Lord, show me...

_____

_____

_____

Date: _____

Name 3 dinnertime foods
you are grateful for:

1. _____

2. _____

3. _____

Verse of the Day

❝ And whatever you do, in word or in deed, do everything in the name of the Lord Jesus, giving thanks to the Father through him.

Colossians 3:17 CSB

What does God want to show you from the verse of the day?

Prayer

God, thank you for the time my family gets to spend together. Help me to do all things as if I am doing them for you.

Amen.

My Prayer

God, I can do a better job at...

Date: _____

Name 3 people you have helped
that you are grateful for:

1. _____

2. _____

3. _____

Verse of the Day

" Now faith is confidence in what we hope for and assurance about what we do not see.

Hebrews 11:1 NIV

What does God want to show you from the verse of the day?

___

___

___

Prayer

God, thank you for the faith I have in you. Help me to deepen my belief and help me to rely on you more.

Amen.

My Prayer

God, help me rely on you for...

___

___

___

Date: _____

Name 3 reasons you are
grateful for your legs:

1. _____

2. _____

3. _____

Verse of the Day

❝ Love the Lord your God with all your heart and with all your soul and with all your strength.

Deuteronomy 6:5 NIV

What does God want to show you from the verse of the day?

_____

_____

_____

Prayer

Lord, thank you for all the places my legs can take me to. Help me to appreciate and take care of my body, it is a gift from you.

Amen.

My Prayer

Lord, I can show my love for you more by...

_____

_____

_____

Date: _____

What are 3 books
you are grateful for:

1. _____

2. _____

3. _____

Verse of the Day

❝ Love is patient, love is kind. Love does not envy, is not boastful, is not arrogant, is not rude, is not self-seeking, is not irritable, and does not keep a record of wrongs.

1 Corinthians 13:4-5 CSB

What does God want to show you from the verse of the day?

_____

_____

_____

Prayer

God, thank you for showing me how to love others. Help me to be patient, kind, and keep no records of wrongs for the people in my life.

Amen.

My Prayer

God, forgive me for being impatient with...

_____

Help me to...

_____

_____

Date: _____

Write 3 things that make you happy and you are grateful for:

1. _____
2. _____
3. _____

Verse of the Day

❝ *Remember this—a farmer who plants only a few seeds will get a small crop. But the one who plants generously will get a generous crop. You must each decide in your heart how much to give. And don't give reluctantly or in response to pressure. 'For God loves a person who gives cheerfully.*

2 Corinthians 9:6-7 NLT

What does God want to show you from the verse of the day?

_____

_____

Prayer

God, thank you for generously giving me all that I have. Help me give to others, with a joyful heart, when they are in need.

Amen.

My Prayer

God, when I think about giving, the person that comes to mind is…

_____

I will…

_____

Date: _____

Name 3 ways you show
that you are grateful:

1. _____

2. _____

3. _____

Verse of the Day

> Gentle words are a tree of life; a deceitful tongue crushes the spirit.
>
> Proverbs 15:4 NLT

What does God want to show you from the verse of the day?

_____

_____

_____

Prayer

Lord, thank you for telling me who I am, that I am dearly loved, forgiven, and set apart. Help me to say things to others that will build them up.
Amen.

My Prayer

God, the person I will say something nice to is...

_____

I will tell them...

_____

Date: _____

Write 3 reasons you are grateful for this year:

1. _____
2. _____
3. _____

Verse of the Day

" We can't allow ourselves to get tired of living the right way. Certainly, each of us will receive [everlasting life] at the proper time, if we don't give up. Whenever we have the opportunity, we have to do what is good for everyone, especially for the family of believers.

Galatians 6:9-10 GW

What does God want to show you from the verse of the day?

_____

_____

_____

Prayer

God, thank you for helping me do things that will help others. Help me to see the needs of others and guide me to offer help to them, just like you would.

Amen.

My Prayer

God, I will help...

_____

_____

Date: _____

What are 3 qualities about yourself
that you are grateful God gave you:

1. _____

2. _____

3. _____

Verse of the Day

> *Some [rely] on chariots and others on horses, but we will boast in the name of the LORD our God.*
>
> Psalm 20:7 GW

What does God want to show you from the verse of the day?

_____

_____

_____

Prayer

Lord, thank you for the ways you have made me special. Help me to remember that the things I am good at are gifts from you. Help me to use the gifts you have blessed me with to bless others.

Amen.

My Prayer

God, one of the things I love about you is...

_____

_____

_____

Date: _____

What are 3 things you love that you are grateful for:

1. _____

2. _____

3. _____

Verse of the Day

" Pay careful attention to your own work, for then you will get the satisfaction of a job well done, and you won't need to compare yourself to anyone else.

Galatians 6:4 NLT

What does God want to show you from the verse of the day?

_____

_____

_____

Prayer

God, thank you for the people I love dearly in my life. Help me focus on you so I can get my approval from you, while not comparing myself to others.

Amen.

My Prayer

God, I compare myself to...

_____

Help me to...

_____

Date: _____

Name 3 furry or fuzzy
things you are grateful for:

1. _____

2. _____

3. _____

Verse of the Day

❝ But be sure to fear the LORD and serve him faithfully with all your heart; consider what great things he has done for you.

1 Samuel 12:24 NIV

What does God want to show you from the verse of the day?

_____

_____

_____

Prayer

Lord, thank you for all the great things you have done for me in my life. Help me to fully understand that all good and perfect things are gifts that come from you.

Amen.

My Prayer

Lord, I need your help to understand why...

_____

_____

_____

Date: _____

Name 3 Bible stories
that you are grateful for:

1. _____

2. _____

3. _____

Verse of the Day

❝ All Scripture is inspired by God and is useful to teach us what is true and to make us realize what is wrong in our lives. It corrects us when we are wrong and teaches us to do what is right.

2 Timothy 3:16 NLT

What does God want to show you from the verse of the day?

_____

_____

_____

Prayer

God, thank you for giving me the Bible as a guide. Help me to correct the things that are wrong in my life.

Amen.

My Prayer

God, forgive me for...

_____

_____

_____

Date: _____

What are 3 ways being grateful makes you feel:

1. _____

2. _____

3. _____

Verse of the Day

❝ *The Spirit himself testifies with our spirit that we are God's children.*

Romans 8:16 ISV

What does God want to show you from the verse of the day?

_____

_____

_____

Prayer

God, thank you for giving me the Holy Spirit. Help me to set aside quiet time to listen to your guidance.

Amen.

My Prayer

God, you tell me that I am...

_____

_____

_____

Date: _____

Write 3 experiences
you are grateful for:

1. _____

2. _____

3. _____

Verse of the Day

> 'Go out and stand before me on the mountain,' the LORD told him. And as Elijah stood there, the LORD passed by, and a mighty windstorm hit the mountain. It was such a terrible blast that the rocks were torn loose, but the LORD was not in the wind. After the wind there was an earthquake, but the LORD was not in the earthquake. And after the earthquake there was a fire, but the LORD was not in the fire. And after the fire there was a sound of a gentle whisper.

1 Kings 19:11-12 NLT

What does God want to show you from the verse of the day?

_____

_____

_____

Prayer

Lord, thank you for stories like this, stories that show me your great power. Help me to set time aside time to listen for your gentle whispers.

Amen.

My Prayer

Lord, I can make time to listen to your voice by...

_____

_____

_____

Date: _____

What are 3 things found in the sky that you are grateful for:

1. _____
2. _____
3. _____

Verse of the Day

❝ You fathers- if your children ask for a fish, do you give them a snake instead? Or if He asks for an egg, do you give them a scorpion? Of course not! If you then, who are evil, know how to give good gifts to your children, how much more will your heavenly Father give the Holy Spirit to those who ask him!

Luke 11:11-13 ESV

What does God want to show you from the verse of the day?

_____

_____

_____

Prayer

God, thank you for the gift of the Holy Spirit. Help me turn to you in prayer when I am frustrated, sad, stressed, happy, and joyful. In my good times and bad.

Amen.

My Prayer

God, a hard situation where I need your help is…

_____

_____

_____

Date: _____

Name 3 people you saw last week that you are grateful for:

1. _____

2. _____

3. _____

Verse of the Day

> Then the Lord God formed a man of dust from the ground, and breathed into his nostrils the breath of life; and man, became a living being.

Genesis 2:7 NASB

What does God want to show you from the verse of the day?

_____

_____

_____

Prayer

Lord, thank you for my family and friends. Help me to remember that everything good comes from you, including the people I love.

Amen.

My Prayer

God, help me to...

_____

_____

Date: _____

What are 3 things you listen to that you are grateful for:

1. _____

2. _____

3. _____

Verse of the Day

> Finally, brothers, whatever is true, whatever is honorable, whatever is fair, whatever is pure, whatever is acceptable, whatever is commendable, if there is anything of excellence and if there is anything praiseworthy—keep thinking about these things.

Philippians 4:8 ISV

What does God want to show you from the verse of the day?

_____

_____

_____

Prayer

God, thank you for giving us ears to hear and a mind to think. Help me think about and listen to things that are pleasing to you.

Amen.

My Prayer

God, help me re-focus my thoughts on your goodness when I start thinking about…

_____

_____

_____

Date: _____

Name 3 things that happened
yesterday that you are grateful for:

1. _____

2. _____

3. _____

Verse of the Day

> But I am like a green olive tree in the house of God. I trust in the steadfast love of God forever and ever.

Psalm 52:8 ESV

What does God want to show you from the verse of the day?

_____

_____

_____

Prayer

God, thank you that your love lasts forever and ever. Help me to be a light for you, so that your love can change the way I treat others.

Amen.

My Prayer

God, help me to love...

_____

By...

_____

Date: _____

What are 3 holidays
that you are grateful for:

1. _____

2. _____

3. _____

Verse of the Day

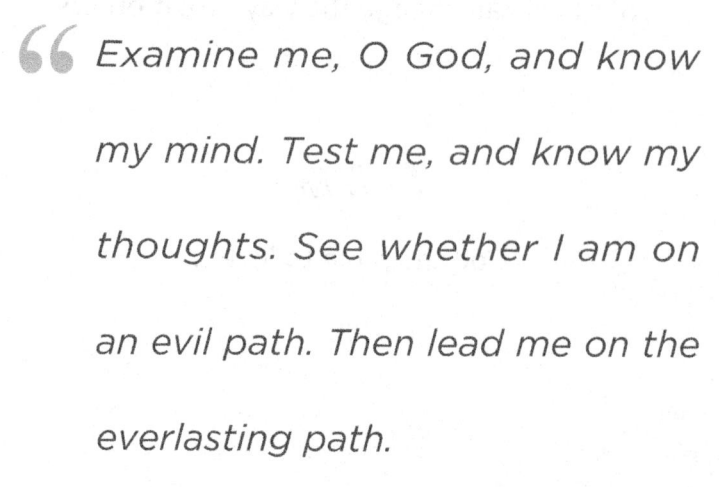

> *Examine me, O God, and know my mind. Test me, and know my thoughts. See whether I am on an evil path. Then lead me on the everlasting path.*
>
> Psalm 139:23-24 GW

What does God want to show you from the verse of the day?

_____

_____

_____

Prayer

God, thank you for the fun I have had during the holidays. Help me to keep everything in my life in order. Above all, help me to keep you first.

Amen.

My Prayer

God, something I do and know that I shouldn't is...

_____

_____

Help me...

_____

Date: _____

Write 3 reasons you are grateful for this journal:

1. _____

2. _____

3. _____

Verse of the Day

> But he told me: 'My kindness is all you need. My power is strongest when you are weak.' So I will brag even more about my weaknesses in order that Christ's power will live in me.

2 Corinthians 12:9 GW

What does God want to show you from the verse of the day?

_____

_____

_____

Prayer

God, thank you for helping me when I am weak. Help me to pray without ceasing and spend time with you when I feel discouraged and weak.

Amen.

My Prayer

God, I feel weak when...

_____

Help me to...

_____

_____

Date: _____

Write 3 things you do when
you're having fun:

1. _____

2. _____

3. _____

Verse of the Day

❝ *He who conceals his sins doesn't prosper, but whoever confesses and renounces them find mercy.*

Proverbs 28:13 WEB

What does God want to show you from the verse of the day?

_____

_____

_____

Prayer

God, thank you for forgiving me of all my sins. Help me to confess my sins and follow your ways each time I make a mistake.

Amen.

My Prayer

God, a sin I need to confess is...

_____

_____

_____

Date: _____

Name 3 warm things
you are grateful for:

1. _____
2. _____
3. _____

Verse of the Day

❝ *But the Lord said to Samuel, 'Don't judge by his appearance or height, for I have rejected him. The LORD doesn't see things the way you see them. People judge by outward appearance, but the LORD looks at the heart.'*

1 Samuel 16:7 NLT

What does God want to show you from the verse of the day?

_____

_____

_____

Prayer

Lord, help me not to like or dislike others because of how they seem on the outside. Help me see others by their character, just as you do.

Amen.

My Prayer

God, I have judged or said mean things about...

_____

Help me to...

_____

_____

Date: _____

Name 3 things that make you cold that you are grateful for:

1. _____

2. _____

3. _____

Verse of the Day

> With the tongue we bless our Lord and Father, and with it we curse people who are made in God's likeness. Blessing and cursing come out of the same mouth. My brothers and sisters, these things should not be this way.

James 3:9-10 CSB

What does God want to show you from the verse of the day?

_____

_____

_____

Prayer

Lord, thank you for giving me verses like this, it tells me exactly how to act and react. Help me to speak only good things to others.

Amen.

My Prayer

Lord, help me see the goodness in...

_____

_____

_____

Date: _____

Write 3 reasons you
are grateful today:

1. _____

2. _____

3. _____

Verse of the Day

" But the fruit of the Spirit is love, joy, peace, patience, kindness, goodness, faithfulness, gentleness, self-control; against such things there is no law.

Galatians 5:22 ESV

What does God want to show you from the verse of the day?

_____

_____

_____

Prayer

Thank you for all the blessings that come from your Spirit. Help me grow in the areas I am not good at.

Amen.

My Prayer

God, I pray that your Spirit gives me more…

_____

_____

_____

CONGRATULATIONS!!!!!

YOU MADE IT THROUGH 90 ENTRIES OF GRATITUDE AND DEVOTIONALS.

I hope God moved in mighty ways while you were completing your journal.

I pray that you can now see God for who He is, others through His eyes and yourself as the marvelous creation He made you to be.

DON'T STOP HERE.

Visit
www.KidsGratitudeJournals.com
for our newest edition!

Made in the USA
Monee, IL
27 February 2025